INFNITY NETWORK

Infinity Network

JIM JOHNSTONE

THE POETRY IMPRINT AT VÉHICULE PRESS

Published with the generous assistance of the Canada Council for the Arts and the Canada Book Fund of the Department of Canadian Heritage.

SIGNAL EDITIONS EDITOR: CARMINE STARNINO

Cover design by David Drummond
Author photo by Erica Smith
Set in Minion and Filosofia by Simon Garamond
Printed by Marquis Book Printing Inc.

Dépôt légal, Library and Archives Canada and the Bibliothèque national du Québec, second trimester 2022

LIBRARY AND ARCHIVES CANADA CATALOGUING IN PUBLICATION
Title: Infinity network / Jim Johnstone.
Names: Johnstone, Jim, 1978- author.
Description: Poems.
Identifiers: Canadiana (print) 20220152659 | Canadiana (ebook) 20220152675 | ISBN 9781550655971 (softcover) | ISBN 9781550656039 (HTML)
Classification: LCC PS8619.O489 I54 2022 | DDC C811/.6—dc23

Published by Véhicule Press, Montréal, Québec, Canada
www.vehiculepress.com

Distribution in Canada by LitDistCo
www.litdistco.ca

Distributed in the US by Independent Publishers Group
www.ipgbook.com

Printed in Canada on FSC certified paper.

In and of itself, nothing really matters. What matters is that nothing is ever in and of itself.

—CHUCK KLOSTERMAN

CONTENTS

∫

The Ouroboros

Here are the ribs. Here the shoulders, the heart—

> an expanding
> itch

> interrupting
> the body's

symmetry.

> Myself, more or less,
> tattooed

before the black gasp sucks back into the gun,

> paint
> circling

> the barrel's
> darkening

mouth.

> Here are the bronchioles.
> Here the lungs, the throat.

When I wrap my injury and wait for the city
to quiet

        the ink sets.

        My body
        reestablishes its limits.

The Three-Day Blood Drive Begins

with a drip. Welcome.
Those gathered are asked to sit
and extend their sleeves,
clench their fists as if fists

could bring about a flood,
the shift needed
for the national reservoirs
to reach their limit.

Next to the vending machines,
a nurse siphons out life
by the quart. Is it wrong
to take more from those with more

to give? It's need that urges
the nurse to flit
from donor to donor like a moth,
to attend the great silence

of the room with a silence
of his own. And this is Day One.
The room brings the innocent,
brings professionals

to give of their innocence,
brings those who crave
release dolled up in red stickers
and summer dresses.

It takes one hour to save
up to three lives. It took one hour
for us to strap the nurse
to a chair—welcome—

to remove his shoes and socks,
strip his shirt while ejecting
pop from the vending machine.
More to strip him down

completely and cut him open.
What then? A neighborly
greeting? A bloodletting
to end all bloodlettings?

Post-Truth

There is no gospel, no glory
in what we do for the greater good—
not with the two-way mirror
reserved for alternative
facts, the empty pool entered
when we need a fish bowl to rest
in, and resting, urge hangers-
on to chip the paint, strip away
any reminders that we were here,
together, if only just to laugh
off truth—meme, meaning,
identity—the ground floor
where we disguise, despite everything,
as wolves in wolves' clothing.

Trompe L'Oeil

The problem is permission and I told you
I don't like to be touched.

> The problem is
> self-harm—
>
> > knuckles aligned to read:
>
> HATE / LOVE.

The problem is busy defending itself,

> calling out names,
>
> building a brand we can trust.
>
> The problem is
> *Jesus Christ shut up!*

The problem is unexpected freedom

> leading to
> expected resolve.

The problem is being caught in the throes
of passion,

      that all our friends
      now know

      we like to film ourselves
      in the missionary position.

The problem is the problem

        until we make restitutions.

      The problem is
      us,

      not 'them.'

Headphones

I cover my ears and hear the train burrowing
from station to station like a worm,
the budding vows of commuters certain
they've disconnected from the crowd's
drumming, and then, without considering
others around them, saying *watch this*,
saying *it didn't mean anything*,
saying *I've heard that before* before I notice
how calmly the passengers across from me
share their contempt for my choice of seat,
knowing guilt doesn't obey the momentum
of the track carrying us forward
and is lessened when I cover my ears, like this,
or replace my hands with headphones
to catch conversation without consent,
my body stiff, consciousness a wick lit
then relit for all those who ignore privilege,
the faces that might as well be moulded
from tinfoil for all I know of their reflections,
of the passenger side window
and the comets that consume us when we arrive
at gaps in the tunnel, the intersections
where we glimpse the outside world,
the trapeze and tightening trapezius

of those who leave while we warm our hands
and continue to fall through space,
do you remember, what someone must have called
the great equalizer, the only place
where we'd be forced to admit
that we hadn't just been unfair to each other,
there was more, and that eventually safety
would be torn away like a cover
scrutinized instead of the book it was designed
to represent, the stories about space camp,
astronauts in tinfoil running
from screen-sized lizards where even Odysseus
failed to land, even sound, the assumed
satisfaction of bass and drums
locked in my head, failed to send, and deadened
so I could listen in, and listening
give up my seat when a new set of bodies
floods past, arms raised in relief
saying *I can't believe how hard she's fighting it*,
saying *they're so brave*, and then what
I've been waiting for, lower, a voice repeating
the words tattooed on my arm:
     We belong dead
as if I'd recognized my name for the first time,
the source of my ID,
trespass beat, beat, beating in my brain.

Identity as an Infinity Mirror

*By translating hallucinations and fear of
hallucinations into paintings, I have been
trying to cure my disease.*

—YAYOI KUSAMA

Each body, an entrance

each entrance
a syllable

      repeating

until variations
appear.

      Here.

      Here
and here
and here.

■

The first cut is a cure—
skin seamed

        and re-
   seamed

like the sleeve
of a wedding dress.

■

Canker.
Cancer.

■

Uninterested in 'I,' or the eye's interior.

Uninterested in hallucinations, fear.

Uninterested in circumspection.

Uninterested in the held, holding, missing.

Uninterested in another version.

Uninterested in pride when pride is at hand.

Uninterested in 'right'.

Uninterested in the element of surprise.

■

Here and here and here and here and here and here
here and here and here and here and here and here
here and here and here and here and here and here
here and here and here and here and here and here
here and here and here and here and here and here
here and here and here and here and here and here
here and here and here and here and here and here
here and here and here and here and here and here
here and here and here and here and here and here
here and here and here and here and here and here
here and here and here and here

■

There are those who don't understand
this condition—

the 'something'
in 'we've all got to die of something.'

The Outrage Industry

We can work around ignorance.
We can even work around the truth.
In spite of built-in defenses, admit
you've been abusive and the abused
will lift the statute of limitations
on sin. Or better yet, kneel in front
of a jury of your peers: talisman;
lynch mob; lashing tail. A whip
pummeling screens until they fill
with TV snow. You can almost switch
the channel but the mirror wall
is black light. Let me tell you more…
no, let me tell you that the more we talk,
the more I'm convinced I'm right.

Speaking Distance

Queen's Park, Toronto

I follow a gull to a bench near the park's gates
and sit down to read a magazine. If you cut
through my line of sight, the pages between us will fall
like artillery, like the spears that frame the southern wall
of the Assembly. I see the same faces each time
I come visit, say *hello*, maybe *the thing is*,
and conversation holds true. But even when caught in a lie
I'd rather speak than be spoken to.

This morning, the leaves drop quietly, drop together
until the ground limits their congregation.
Space to heal. I was happy before I distracted
a cyclist riding past the sculpture of Al Purdy
and I was happy when they fell. It's not enough
that the poet couldn't shut up in his lifetime—
now his bronze body is disguised in a Jays cap.
In fact, his body is positively chiseled—

the kind of figure that stands for *the whole story*,
though in his case we have to fill in the gaps. I'm rarely
sure, but can imagine the look on the cyclist's
face—you know the one—as if I'd sucked the air
out of the park after he refused to speak up for himself.
And there, on the ground, pausing to see who'll play the hero,
the two of us watch a bird fly into outlines
of larger birds stuck on the Assembly's windows.

Heaven Spot

*Graffiti belongs in the streets. One of the best
things about it is that it doesn't last—it resists
ownership.*

—ANSER

A line, a lip, a like-
ness reclaimed
in particulate,
paint masking paint,

the climb, the taint
of efflorescent
tags overcome
when dropping the mic.

The Mirror Wall

                   contains multitudes.

More than birds
of a feather,

                   the reconfiguration
                   of wing and wire,

the mirror wall contains every copy
of a copied

                   room,

every hall that hails
the entrance

of the living living in perfect sprawl.

Visible in peak
sunlight,

                   shapeshifters all.

Identity as a Wormhole in a Hotel Window

The style is to stand out. Beard grown past
the Adam's apple, neighbours barking
at streetlights like startled dogs.
I bark along. Having tried to buy cigarettes
with half a five dollar bill—the other half
lost when rain divided the town—
I find myself on the outside of a hotel
looking in. Look in and Main wormholes
away from the street's sporadic yellow line:
cars on the east side of the median wet,
beaded with salt and sun sponged
from the lobby's darkening border. I can
feel the sky getting closer. Anyone
with good taste stays dry, drives out
(instead of into) town, and having grown
tired of *no* I pass my chunk of Laurier's
head off to a friend looking to play god.
Identity is fluid. The bill's new steward
spins an orange and red umbrella at her side,
the day weaponized, clouds pooling
like a flag beneath the hotel's vacancy sign.
In time, others gather to throw their bad
teeth into the black hole's widening
mouth, to hear the girl with the umbrella
tell them that whatever is going to happen
has already happened. Is history. The news-
cast where protestors are roundly shouted
down. *You little fucks!* The words sting all
of us, but who here is prepared to be patient,

to grow suddenly five years older
and start waiting on the moneyed
guests? Identity is a spell that inverts
our reflections before coming to rest. One day
the barking will stop—then restart
in the present tense. One day everyone
who rents a room in this town will be different.

pass my ch
to a friend looking
tity is fluid. The bill's new s
ns an orange and red umbrella
e day weaponized, clouds poolin
ke a flag beneath the hotel's vacan
time, others gather to throw the
th into the black hole's widenin
th, to hear the girl with the
m that whatever is goi
happened. Is

Deleted Scenes

1

Overturned, a turkey buzzard
will rest in your hand.

Cut out its beak.
Cut out its circling calm.

The once loved
will run through what's next—

would,
should.

Before they lift the feathers.
Before they go off script.

2

I set out, toe to tail, whistling
into the oncoming crowd.

Not me exactly—
my sense of self.

Black book broken at the spine,
thinning hair.

Shame scavenging
then settling over all—

both whistler and whistled-at,
I solemnly swear.

3

The buzzard clears its throat.
Give pause.

Pause for snow to explode
like a downed shuttlecock.

Pause to split a wishbone
at the mudroom's groove.

Once there, leather
smoothes every available wing.

Vandalism a letter-
based form of alienation.

4

Your body is serious
and it's your body I prefer.

Quiet.
Who's there?

Silent summer, silent footing,
silent square.

I would help if I were present,
if the past weren't ignored.

You'll know my face
by the way it answers yours.

5

Sober again. Don't listen to me
in this state.

Conscious enough to develop
fever, blister from sheer depravity.

Stop that. Again, *stop that
or I'll start to shout.*

Moss, thistle, vetch.
Phlox, hogweed, pine.

The neon lines that border the dance
floor remain undanced upon.

6

Can't,
won't.

The buzzard's tongue stretches
right out, like a bridge.

Slats pulled, fat lip
jingling from suspended jaws.

When our mouths heal
we'll take a course corrected path.

The buzzard's tongue unrolled,
stand-in for the change we want.

7

It wasn't me who yelled at you
earlier. It was

but it wasn't.
That's all over now.

Nothing less
than an itch beneath you.

When I finally come home
I'll be skinned to the bone.

Tongue-tied.
The first words that come to mind.

8

When the mouth's full, the mind
twists the tongue's prosody.

The flak,
the flesh.

I dream a stolen, split-eyed path.
I do despise my dream.

Waddling wedding-cans
announce the impending blast.

Attack,
attain, refresh.

9

I unzip and adjust my screen—
a pop-up blocks

the pornography.
Now look through new eyes.

A leather belt
becomes another rib.

Tabs clear and we share
a common language.

I unzip and unzip and unzip
and unzip.

Rise, already. Rise and wad
your words with rubber bands.

A cheap trick getting cheaper
by the minute.

Never?
Until.

The fleeting feeling
of an unanswered punch.

The sky compressed
like an empty sponge.

Performance Anxiety

I write: *the tall grass is a third wish*

then back away

from the field. If I move
back

far enough, everyone in the front
row will be still.

Be still—
you're witnessing my first time.

A ballooning ballroom expanding

until the beat drops,
a letdown

letting you down gently

before the DJ jumps up, afraid to play
something that could offend.

I write: *the tall grass is a third wish*
wasted

and pray

for more wishes as the grasslands end.

Radio Silence

Before rain begins to burn the sidewalk
spring corrects into summer,
becomes the whip that steadies
the family offering tainted meat
to off-leash pets—a downturned hand,
then another spilling antifreeze
the colour of the ocean seen from space.
The youngest orbits the block
telling those who'll listen
that they're already dead—surrogates
who'd gladly donate the spider-web
of their bodies to be among the saved.
And what of the others? Have they
yielded to calm, or do they break
the silence like insects droning
through the single day they've been given
to live? It's bloodlust connects us
and bloodlust that fills the neighbourhood
as the afternoon dies down
to radio silence, washes over the family
that believes in itself, wholly,
refusing to admit that each member
exists in their own, increasingly effortless hell.

It's 1978

It's 1978   The meaning of "stand still"
is "wait."

It's 1986   The national anthem plays
from a thousand
King Kong cassette decks.

It's 1999   I walk out of my home-
town and find
an adjoining suburb burning.

It's 1993   Before year's end,
time is common property.

It's 2004   A stranger follows me
into the cold

and loiters behind a triplex
in their underwear.

It's 1984   The revolution is over.

It's 2001   I'm desperate, and on Sunday
mornings
I swim alone.

It's 2009   The Three-Day Blood Drive fails,
                 despite best laid plans.

It's 1982   *Tonight, they're closing up the world.*

It's 2022   I'm alive as you are.

Identity as an Echo Chamber

If there's room enough in this room to listen,
to hear every available voice speak,
then let's meet in the corner
and work our way out through avatars
of blood and bone, wards that urge
us to redistribute toward open borders.

We can't help but see things as we are,
recoil from strangers who absent-mindedly
flip their safeties and jam their trigger
fingers down, entirely happy to squeeze off
a round before answering to authority.
Then it's all

> *I'm so sorry*,
> or *I couldn't see*,

not with a wallet standing-in for the victim's
hand. As if to look past the body
I log on and confirm I'm right—
we need more ways to protect ourselves.
I say ourselves but I really mean me,
my place in the world, and all that's tangible

from the point of view beamed into my eyes.
You do you. I'll apologize,
but who wouldn't atone
to hear what they want to hear—
that justice preempts firepower,
airspace, the right to get it right another day.

Pornography

Not exactly love—immodesty's

      threat to mean,

demean. Not the hard drive wired

      to mimic sweat,

      the downpour
      of surveillance blinking

out. Not the rub, the shame,

      the swell.

Not the display

      where skin approaches
      as a single
      flag

      and moves towards the DSL.

More like a laying on of hands.

Touch going steady

      with the floor where
      a pill case lands

      and draws everyone down,

down to their knees
to share in its hemorrhage—

Infinity Network

We're safe everywhere until we're not.
In the boardroom, a wall of photographs
compliments the boss's collection of toys,
their custom eyes switched on as I'm told
to draw an X over a new employee's face.
Matt lasted a day, but is mounted
on the whiteboard as if his portrait
might boost morale. In his continued
presence, I'm never alone. On Friday,
when the boss is late, a train of bodies
glides through HQ fighting for my attention
like a bridal party snatching at a bouquet.
I don't play favorites. Tasked with firing
Chris, I'm a good dog, *good boy,*
now go sit on your mat. I wait for an escort
to shepherd her from the building
before jotting the X, only smaller this time,
to imitate the scar on Patricia Krenwinkel's
forehead. If you look hard enough
you'll notice that others have joined her,
that those still working shake and slow.
A cult of runaways—our leader the break
that brightens the brick. At day's end
the room is lit with his selfie stick.
The room is obscured but I'm right here.
Take my photograph so I can disappear.

Don't Look, We're Being Watched

in the same lens where we watch
others, their faces ill-

defined, pixelated,

the window in the top right hand
corner of the screen

extending

its grip. *See?* Pores and palms,
spit filling an elephant cage,

or maybe the jaws

of self same elephant come back,
all stealth, spite

in spite

of its enormity. *Here, take
the webcam and speak clearly*

(blue in a blue streak)

*but find your shadow
before assuming you're experiencing*

déjà vu.

Don't look, but do.

Identity as a Reproducible Method

$$U(t) = U(0) \cdot \frac{k^{\left(\frac{t}{p}+1\right)} - 1}{k - 1}$$

The virus is permission.

The virus is touch.

The virus evolves
      as long as
      it's contagious.

The virus is *go ahead*—
the virus goes ahead
      and spreads
      its envelope.

The virus copies itself.

The virus is the virus
      as long as
      it spares its host.

To Carthage Then We Came

To deny sight is to lay an ear to rail,
its couplings—white noise ringing
in flange that steadies the line,
the echo that frames the city's arrival.
We choose no kin but adopted
strangers, a coda of arms
that level the skin on a passenger's
neck, the lineaments that linger

as they're divided, sense by sense.
Past eight Union's platform rises
to meet the rush of bodies paused
in daylight's corneal scratch—they pass
in an arc of sweat, sibilant disarray—
not the ground, but our legs moving away.

Two Sleep Through

the night, the lowering
balloon that stills
the chop and spill
of the lake, one awake,
or awake enough
in dream to follow
the stink of a fox
through the trees,
two asleep where the last
of a bonfire burns
the beach, balloons
into thought
without articulation,
without speech,
one awake, brightening
behind the bathroom
door while the other
waits, listens to the tap
foam foam foaming
at the mouth, white noise
drowning out the fox,
the fire, the balloon
inflating until it pops.

The Ouroboros (Reprise)

Here's the city. Here the empty pool, the chorus

        of commuters
        making their way

        to the wall,

walled in

            while infusing a wound.

            The wall
            is an emptying—

a city block
upturned

        to shake

exact and endless onlookers

        off the paint,

                the pavement.

The wall defines our lack of sovereignty.

You
        and I

and everyone else
who isn't.

        Isn't permanent

or part
        of the panoply.

Beyond the gates the only sound is the excited

        breathing
of two dogs.

The rest have run out.

Run past

        boundaries marked
        with indomethacin,

boundaries marked
by sparrows,

    pigeons,

the pride
of urban-based evolution.

Have you heard this?

         The wall is a whisper campaign—

homesick,

        housing the sick
        and the testament

of illness.

        Recovery and constraint.

This island.

This chest, beat.

         Over and over.

Beat.

The city is four walls, the mouth of a gargoyle

        presiding over tenants,
        tenements,

winged brick

and beaks
of see-through glass.

        If shouts were music
        the whole world would be singing

        Don't ruin it.
        Don't ruin it.
        Don't ruin it.

        Singing
        the black gasp sucks back into the gun,

a deep breath
        oxygenating walls,

        approximating ribs,

                the body rendered in paint,

breathing in,

        marked

safe until

safety is questioned.

There is no
question.

Scab. Scarab.

Everything safely shared
between
neighbours

before the land
is cleared.

In the clearing,
fireworks arch over city hall.

Archangel and enemy,

parliament elected to ensure
we finish

what we started.

Nail sculptures,
talk
        and talk's positive charge

        lassoed

around

            the city's limits.

Tagged, triggered, targeted.

The black gasp

        sucks

the black
      gasp

        sucks

back

in sight of the sovereign state—
a place

        (like any other place)

where the way
though

stands-in for formal
invitation.

Deformed mouth. Mouth with the tail of a snake

trailing

its own

tongue.

Inexorable.

Incoming.

The city is in motion.

You've reached the wall

written on the wall once
you reach

the ocean.

NOTES

"Headphones" references Ken Babstock's description of the Toronto subway as a "civic worm" in *Airstream Land Yacht* (House of Anansi Press, 2006).

The epigraph to "Heaven Spot" is taken from a February 26, 2014 interview with Anser published in NOW magazine.

"It's 1978" incorporates lyrics from "Car Jamming" by The Clash.

"Identity as a Reproducible Method" is prefaced by the equation for viral growth as a function of time.

"To Carthage Then We Came" incorporates lyrics from "Three Days" by Jane's Addiction. It was written in response to the G-20 Summit protest that took place in Toronto, Ontario, in 2010.

ACKNOWLEDGMENTS

My thanks to the editors of the following publications where poems in *Infinity Network* previously appeared:

32 Poems (US): "Two Sleep Through"

Acumen (UK): "Radio Silence"

Arc Poetry Magazine: "Deleted Scenes 6, 7, 8, 10," "The Mirror Wall" and "The Three-Day Blood Drive Begins"

Canadian Literature: "To Carthage Then We Came"

Canadian Medical Association Journal: "Identity as a Reproducible Method"

The Dalhousie Review: "Deleted Scenes 1-3"

Envoi (UK): "Post-Truth"

Grain: "Infinity Network"

Literary Review of Canada: "Headphones" and "Identity as an Echo Chamber"

Magma (UK): "It's 1978"

New Contrast (SA): "Identity as a Wormhole in a Hotel Window" and "Trompe L'Oeil"

Poetry (US): "Performance Anxiety"

Poetry Salzburg Review (AT): "Don't Look, We're Being Watched" and "The Ouroboros"

Prairie Fire: "Identity as an Infinity Mirror"

The Walrus: "Heaven Spot" and "The Outrage Industry"

"Speaking Distance" and "To Carthage Then We Came" were anthologized in *Resisting Canada: An Anthology of Poetry* (Véhicule Press, 2019).

"Identity as an Infinity Mirror" won the 2018 Bliss Carman Poetry Award.

"The Ouroboros (Reprise)" was shortlisted for the 2019 Robin Blaser Poetry Award, and was printed as a pamphlet by Knife | Fork | Book.

My thanks to the Canada Council of the Arts and the Ontario Arts Council for funding that sustained me while writing this book.

ALSO BY THE AUTHOR

Poetry

The Velocity of Escape (2008)
Patternicity (2010)
Sunday, the locusts (2011)
Dog Ear (2014)
The Chemical Life (2017)

Chapbooks

Siamese Poems (2006)
Epoch (2013)
Microaggressions (2016)
The Ouroboros (2021)

Anthologies

The Next Wave: An Anthology of 21st Canadian Poetry (2018)

As Editor

The Essential Earle Birney (2014)
The Essential D. G. Jones (2016)

Stephen Scobie • Peter Dale Scott • Deena Kara Shaffer
Carmine Starnino • Andrew Steinmetz • David Solway
Ricardo Sternberg • Shannon Stewart
Philip Stratford, trans. • Matthew Sweeney
Harry Thurston • Rhea Tregebov • Peter Van Toorn
Patrick Warner • Derek Webster • Anne Wilkinson
Donald Winkler, trans. • Shoshanna Wingate
Christopher Wiseman • Catriona Wright
Terence Young